The Farty Joke Book!

belongs to

____

Other **Red Fox** *joke books*

THE SMELLY SOCKS JOKE BOOK by Susan Abbott

THE EVEN SMELLIER SOCKS JOKE BOOK by Karen King

THE BULLYBUSTERS JOKE BOOK by John Byrne

SANTA'S CHRISTMAS JOKE BOOK by Katie Wales

THE GOOD EGG YOLK BOOK by Katie Wales

BEST BROWNIE JOKES by Brownies

BEST CUB JOKES by Cub Scouts

THE SCHOOL RULES JOKE BOOK by Karen King

THE MILLENNIUM JOKE BOOK by Sue Mongredien

THE FISH 'N' CHIPS JOKE BOOK by Ian Rylett

AMAZING ANIMAL JOKES by John Hegarty

THE FAT CAT JOKE BOOK by Susan Abbot

THE NUTTY INTERNET JOKE BOOK by John Byrne

THE FUNNIEST JOKE BOOK IN THE WORLD EVER

U. SMELL

Cover and illustrations by
Garry Davis

RED FOX

A Red Fox Book

Published by Random House Children's Books
20 Vauxhall Bridge Road, London SW1V 2SA

A division of The Random House Group Ltd
London Melbourne Sydney Auckland
Johannesburg and agencies throughout the world

3 5 7 9 10 8 6 4

Typeset by SX Composing DTP, Rayleigh, Essex
Printed and bound in Great Britain by
Bookmarque Ltd, Croydon, Surrey

THE RANDOM HOUSE GROUP Limited Reg No. 954009

www.randomhouse.co.uk

ISBN 0 09 941380 9

CONTENTS

FOUL FARTS

My old man's a dustman,
He wears a dustman's hat,
He farted through the keyhole,
And paralysed the cat.
The dog went through the window,
He couldn't stand the smell,
My old man's a dustman,
And he can fart dead well.

Laugh and the world laughs with
you, fart and you stand alone.

What's invisible and
 smells like carrots?
Rabbit farts.

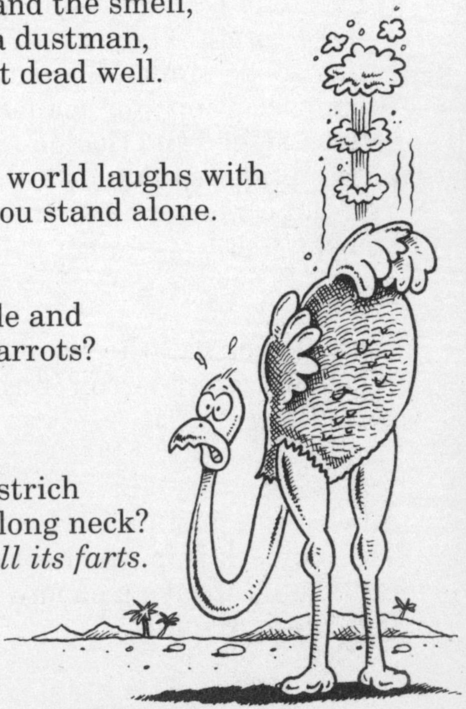

Why does an ostrich
 have such a long neck?
So it can't smell its farts.

What's brown and sounds like a bell?
Dung.

'Doctor, you've got to help me. I can't stop farting,' said the patient.

The doctor nodded. 'Hmm!'

'I fart all the time,' said the patient. 'My farts don't smell and you can't hear them. See, I've been here five minutes and I've farted several times but you didn't hear me or smell them, did you?'

The doctor looked thoughtful. 'Hmm.' He picked up his pen and started writing a prescription.

'Oh good,' smiled the patient. 'Will the prescription stop me farting?'

'No,' sighed the Doctor. 'This prescription is to unblock your nose. You can come back tomorrow for a hearing test.'

What do you call the smelliest and hairiest royal person in the world?
King Pong.

A belch is a gust of wind,
That cometh from the heart,
But should it take a downward trend,
It turneth to a fart.

A Japanese man and an American man were playing golf. The Japanese man was just about to hit the ball when he paused and began to talk into his thumb.

'What are you doing?' asked the American, puzzled.

'Don't worry,' said the Japanese man. 'I was just recording a message to the micro-technic dictaphone in my thumb.'

The two men then continued playing golf. Suddenly, the American made a noise that sounded just like a fart. The Japanese man looked over at him.

'Don't worry,' said the American. 'I was just receiving a fax.'

Why did the boy eat so many baked beans?
He wanted to go wind surfing.

What does the Queen do when she burps?
Issues a Royal Pardon.

Why are fried onions like a photocopying machine?
They keep repeating themselves.

A midwife was walking past the hospital staff room when she heard two African doctors talking.

'I'm telling you it's wumba. W-U-M-B-A,' said the first.

'No, no, it's woomba. W-O-O-M-B-A,' said the second.

The midwife popped her head round the door. 'Actually, gentlemen, you're both wrong. It's womb,' she said. 'W-O-M-B.'

The two doctors stared at her, then one said, 'Madam, when did you ever see a water buffalo never mind hear one fart in a mudpool?'

Ma Biggins' café was famous for its bean casserole. Everyone loved it, especially as it didn't make you fart like other bean casseroles did.

After finishing off a huge plateful, one customer said, 'That was delicious, Ma, but why doesn't your bean casserole make you fart?'

'Simple,' replied Ma. 'I always use exactly 239 beans.'

'Why's that?' asked the customer.

'Because,' smiled Ma, 'one more would make it Two Forty!' (*Too Farty*!)

A woman was getting really annoyed because her husband kept farting.

'You should get a job in the meteorology office,' she snapped.

'Why's that?' he asked.

'Because you're an expert on wind!' she retorted.

What do you call someone who never blows his nose?
Ronnie.

What do you do if your nose goes on strike?
Picket.

Derek had a terrible passion for beans. He really loved them but they always made him fart. So when he met a girl he really loved and wanted to marry he decided that he would make the supreme sacrifice and give up beans. Soon afterwards they married and moved to a little cottage in the country and Derek never touched baked beans.

Then, a few months later, Derek was on the way home from work when his car broke down. He phoned his wife to warn her that he'd be late home and set off for the long walk home. On the way he passed a café and smelt the wonderful aroma of baked beans. As he had several miles to walk he thought he could work off the effect of the beans before he got home so he went in the café and ordered three extra large helpings of baked beans. He really enjoyed his feast. All the way back he kept farting a bit so he thought he would be OK by the time he got home.

Derek's wife met him at the door, looking really pleased. 'I've got a lovely surprise for you tonight,' she said. She put a blindfold on him and led him to a chair at the table, making him promise not to speak. Just as his wife went to remove the blindfold the telephone rang. So she made him promise not to peek until she returned and went to answer it.

Derek could feel another fart coming on so as soon as he heard his wife pick up the phone he let it come out. It was really loud and smelt really awful. Then he did another and another. The room smelt so bad he had to grab the napkin off the table and fan himself with it. Just then, Derek heard his wife say goodbye and put the phone down. He folded his napkin and put it back on the table then smiled contentedly. Just in time!

His wife walked back in, apologised for taking so long and removed the blindfold, shouting 'SURPRISE!' And to Derek's shock and horror, there were twelve dinner guests seated around the table . . . for his surprise birthday party!

Why did Captain Kirk go into the ladies' toilet?
To boldly go where no man had gone before.

What do you call someone who doesn't use a hankie?
Greensleeves.

What happened to the man who stole a lorry load of prunes?
He was on the run for a week.

How do you make a tissue dance?
Put a little boogey in it.

Why is basketball so messy?
Because you dribble on the floor.

A man with terrible B.O. walked into the chemist and said, 'I'd like something to take this smell away.'

'So would I, sir,' said the chemist, holding his nose. 'So would I!'

Why did the jogger need so many hankies?
Because his nose was always running.

What do you get if you cross a field with cows in?
A pat on the shoe.

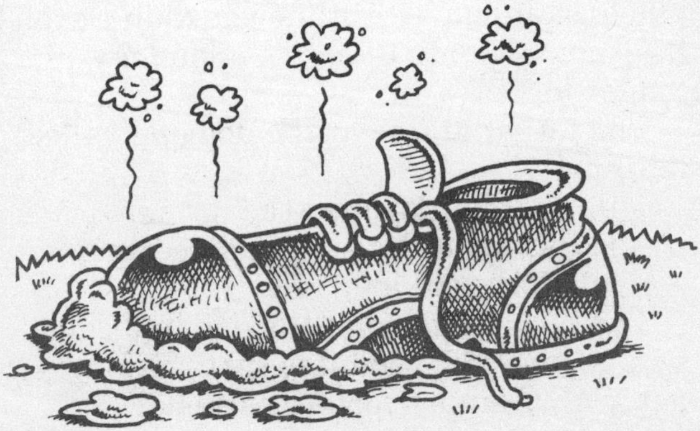

Lenny is so lazy he sticks his nose out the window so the wind will blow it for him.

A woman went to her boyfriend's house for dinner. She'd never met his parents before and was very nervous. As they all sat down for dinner, the woman felt gas pains in her stomach and, try as she might, couldn't help letting out a little fart. It wasn't very loud but everyone heard it. The woman was about to apologise, embarrassed, when the boyfriend's father glared at the dog who had been snoozing at her feet and shouted, sternly, 'Skippy!'

Oh good, they think it was the dog, the woman thought, in relief.

A few minutes later, the woman felt the pains again, and this time she didn't even hesitate. She let out an even louder and longer fart.

The father glared at the dog and yelled, 'Skippy!'

This is great, grinned the woman.

A few minutes later, she farted again. A really long and loud one.

The father looked at the dog in disgust and yelled, 'For goodness sake, Skippy, get away from her before the smell knocks you out!'

Doctor, doctor, I have a lot of wind. Can you give me anything for it?
Certainly, here's a kite.

What do you call a man with cow droppings all over his shoes?
An in cowpoop.

How do you keep vampires away?
Eat garlic-flavoured baked beans and fart all night.

Why do grape harvesters have noses?
So they have something to pick in the growing season.

What do you call a dirty, frayed, hairy, blood-stained thing found on the bathroom floor?
A used elastoplast.

Farty People
Did you know that you can tell what someone is like by the way they fart? Here's a quick guide:
A sporty person farts whenever he does the slightest exercise.

A cheeky person farts out loud then laughs.
An honest person farts, admits it was him but excuses himself with a good, medical explanation.
A shy person farts silently then blushes.
A dishonest person farts then blames the dog.

'There's a terrible smell of B.O. in here,' said the new office boy.

'It's the automatic air-conditioning,' said his boss.

'Automatic air-conditioning?' repeated the boy, looking confused.

'Whenever the weather gets hot it automatically breaks down,' said the boss.

ABOMINABLE ANIMALS

What do worms leave around the top of bath tubs?
The scum of the earth.

Why do giraffes have long necks?
Have you smelt their feet?

How do you keep a fish from smelling?
Cut off its nose.

What's black and green and white and brown?
A cow with a runny nose in a muddy field.

What do you get if you cross an eagle with a skunk?
A bird that stinks to high heaven.

What did the hen say when she saw a scrambled egg?
'There goes my crazy mixed-up kid.'

What do you call a fish that tunes pianos?
A Piano Tuna.

My dog saw a sign
saying 'Wet Paint!'
– so he did!

Little sausage dog,
Crossing the street,
Here comes a motor car,
Now it's sausage meat!

What do you call an insect that's just flown by?
A flu bug.

Why did the elephant eat the candle?
He wanted a light snack.

What fish tastes best with ice cream?
Jellyfish.

Why was the little bird expelled from school?
She was always playing practical yolks.

What do fish take to stay alive?
Vitamin sea.

What is the most musical part of a turkey?
The drumstick.

What lights up the farmyard at night?
A battery hen.

What's smaller than a mosquito's shoe?
A mosquito's foot.

Why did the dog chase its tail?
It was trying to make ends meet.

What do bats sing when it's raining?
Raindrops keep falling on my feet.

Mary had a little lamb,
She also had a horse,
For the horse she made a saddle,
For the lamb she made mint sauce.

What do you call a cow eating grass
in a paddock?
A lawn mooer.

What do you get if you cross a pig with
a dinosaur?
Jurassic Pork.

What creature is useful in a car?
A windscreen viper.

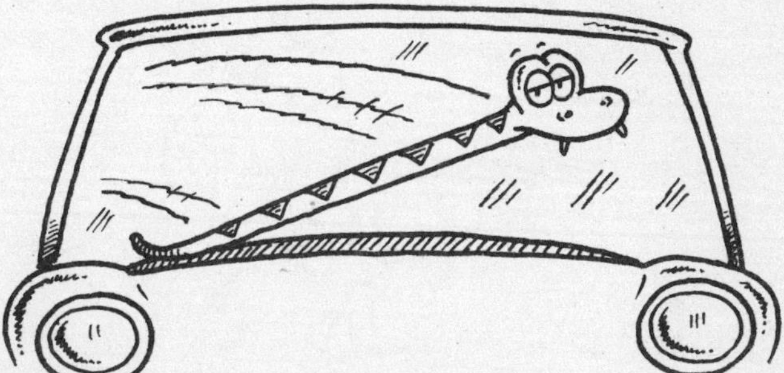

What do you get if you cross a skunk with
a cartoon penguin?
Pingu-Pong.

What do you call a flea that lives in an idiot's ear?
A space invader.

What happened when the cat swallowed a penny?
There was money in the kitty.

There was a young lady called Maggie,
Whose dog was enormous and shaggy,
The front end of him,
Looked vicious and grim,
But the tail end was friendly and waggy.

What did the spider do on the computer?
Make a website.

Why do elephants have wrinkles?
Because they don't like ironing.

What do you get if you cross a bear with a cow pat?
Winnie the Pooh.

What do you get if you cross a chicken with a skunk?
A fowl smell.

What did the skunk say when the wind changed?
It's all coming back to me now!

What did the judge say when the skunk walked into the court room?
Odour in court!

MARY: My budgie keeps laying square eggs!
SUE: That's amazing! Can it talk as well?
MARY: Yes, but only one word.
SUE: What's that?
MARY: Ouch!

What do you get if you cross King Kong with a budgie?
A messy cage.

What kind of disc did the pig put in the computer?
A sloppy disc.

What do you call a sheep with a machine gun?
Lambo.

What does a cat rest his head on?
A caterpillar.

SID: Why do you call your dog Rain?
BERT: Because he makes puddles everywhere.

Which side of a cat has more hair?
The outside.

What do you call two pigs that live together?
Pen pals.

What is the most valuable fish?
The goldfish.

What is the correct name for a water otter?
A kettle.

When is it bad luck for a black cat to cross your path?
When you're a mouse.

What did the cat do when it had swallowed the cheese?
Waited at the mouse hole with baited breath.

What do you get from a pampered cow?
Spoiled milk.

How do fleas travel from place to place?
By itch hiking.

Why did the bird cry?
Because it was a bluebird.

Roses are red,
Violets are pink,
There's an octopus in the bath,
So I'll wash at the sink!

What football team do snakes support?
Slitherpool.

'Why are you feeding money to the cows?'
'Because I want to have rich milk.'

What has one horn and gives fresh milk?
A milk float.

What kind of dog does a scientist have?
A laboratory retriever.

What do you call a flying skunk?
A smellicopter.

What can lizards do that snakes can't?
Stretch their legs.

What sort of cow wears a jumper?
A Jersey.

Why do seagulls live in the sea?
Because if they lived in the bay they'd be bagels.

Why did the ostrich put a net over his head?
Because he wanted to catch his breath.

What part of a fish do we
eat that it doesn't have?
Fish fingers.

Where do baby fish go?
Plaice-school.

A flea and a fly in a flue,
Were trapped so thought what to do,
'Let us fly,' said the flea.
'Let us flee,' said the fly.
So they flew through a flaw in the flue.

Which animals were the last to leave the ark?
The elephants. They were packing their trunks.

Mary had a little lamb,
Its fleece was black as soot,
And everywhere that Mary went,
It's sooty foot it put.

What do you get if you cross a skunk and an owl?
A bird that smells but doesn't give a hoot.

What do you get when you cross a parrot and a centipede?
A walkie-talkie.

What do you get if you cross a worm with a young goat?
A dirty kid.

What do you get if you cross a sheep dog and a bunch of daisies?
Collie-flowers.

How many cockroaches does it take to screw in a light bulb?
You can't tell. As soon as the light comes on they run off!

What do you get when you cross a tyrannosaurus and a skunk?
A stinkasaurus.

Did you hear about the really stupid woodworm?
It was found dead in a housebrick.

What's the difference between a maggot and a cockroach?
Cockroaches crunch more when you eat them.

What dog smells of onions?
A hot dog.

How many skunks does it take to make a big stink?
A phew.

What do you get if you cross a bee with a skunk?
Something that stings and smells.

What do you call a chicken that haunts a house?
A poultry-geist.

If cows get milked what do goats get?
Butted.

What do you get if you cross a cow with a camel?
Lumpy custard.

What is the wettest animal?
A reindeer.

Did you hear about the dog that ate garlic?
His bark was worse than his bite.

Why do the French like snails?
They don't like fast food.

What do we get from naughty cows?
Bad milk.

Where do kangaroos go for an eye test?
The hoptician.

Jack had a bionic cow,
It only ate safety pins,
And every time he milked that cow,
The milk came out in tins.

What do you call a multi-storey pig pen?
A sty-scraper.

Why did the owl make everyone laugh?
Because he was a hoot.

Two cows were talking in a field.
FIRST COW: Are you worried about this mad cow disease?
SECOND COW: Why should I worry about that? I'm a penguin.

What did one maggot say to another?
What's a nice girl like you doing in a joint like this?

Which insect breathes fire?
A dragonfly.

What do you call an Arctic cow?
An Eskimoo.

Why did the elephant paint her head yellow?
To see if blondes really do have more fun.

Why did the turtle cross the road?
To get to the Shell station.

What was the fly doing in the alphabet soup?
Learning to spell.

MANGY MEDICINE

Why did the king go to the dentist?
To have his teeth crowned.

'Why's your son crying?' the doctor asked a young woman in his surgery.

'He has four baked beans stuck up his nose,' she replied.

'And why is his little sister screaming her head off?' asked the doctor.

'She wants the rest of her lunch back!'

What kind of bandage do people wear after heart surgery?
Ticker tape.

Doctor, doctor, my baby is the image of his father.
Never mind, just so long as he is healthy!

A ballerina went to see her doctor.

'Doctor, you must help me,' she cried. 'Every time I pirouette, I fart!'

'Hmm,' murmured the doctor. 'Can you show me?'

So the ballerina stood up, pirouetted and farted loudly.

'Goodness, that's amazing!' gasped the doctor. 'Do it again.'

So the ballerina pirouetted again and farted even louder.

'Hmm, I see what you mean,' said the doctor. 'I think I might be able to help.' He bent down and picked up a long pole with a barbed hook on the end.

The ballerina looked alarmed. 'What are you going to do with that thing?' she gasped.

'Open the window,' replied the doctor. 'It stinks in here!'

Doctor, doctor, my nose keeps running and I don't know what to do.

Stick your feet out in front of you and trip it up.

Which skin complaint comes from London?

Hackney.

Doctor, doctor, some days I feel like a tee-pee and other days I feel like a wig-wam.
You're too tense!

PATIENT: Now tell me honestly, how am I?
DENTIST: Your teeth are fine but your gums have to come out.

Doctor, doctor, I keep dreaming there are huge, horrible monsters playing tiddlywinks under my bed.
What shall I do?
Hide the tiddlywinks.

A bald man came into the doctor's surgery. 'Doctor, can you give me something to cure my baldness?'

'How about a few pounds of pig manure?' suggested the doctor.

'Will that cure my baldness?' asked the man, surprised.

'No,' said the doctor. 'But with that on your head no one will come near enough to know that you're bald.'

Doctor, doctor, I've got a little stye!
Then you'd better buy a little pig.

'I'm sorry,' said the surgeon. 'But I left a sponge in you when I operated last week.'
'So that's why I've been feeling thirsty all the time!' replied the patient.

Doctor, doctor, I keep thinking I'm a mosquito!
Go away, sucker!

Doctor, doctor, I've got athlete's foot in my head.
What makes you think that?
My nose keeps running.

DOCTOR (to smelly patient): You've got the worst B.O. I've ever smelt. I'm afraid that you'll need a major operation.
PATIENT: I'd like a second opinion, please.
DOCTOR (getting closer and taking a big sniff): Yes, you've definitely got the worst B.O. I've ever smelt. You'll need a major operation.

Doctor, doctor, I don't like all these flies buzzing around my head.
Point out the ones you like and I'll swat the rest.

Doctor, doctor, my kidneys are bad. What should I do?
Take them back to the butcher.

Doctor, doctor, I think I'm a python.
You can't get round me just like that, you know!

Doctor, doctor, my wife thinks she's a motorbike.
Give her two of these pills and she'll be cured.
But then how will I get home?

Doctor, doctor, will this ointment clear my spots?
I never make rash promises.

DOCTOR: I'm sorry I can't diagnose the cause of your bad breath. I think it must be the drink.
PATIENT: OK. I'll come back when you're sober.

WOMAN: Doctor, I'm really worried about my little boy's nailbiting habit.
DOCTOR: Don't worry. Nailbiting is very common in children.
WOMAN: What – six inch rusty ones?

Doctor, doctor, I've swallowed a spoon.
Just sit there quietly and don't stir.

Two dentists were discussing a patient. Mr Phang said, 'I wouldn't say his teeth were rotten but every time he stuck his tongue out one of them snapped off.'

MAN: I asked my doctor if he could help me give up smoking.
FRIEND: What did he say?
MAN: He told me that every time I felt like a cigarette I should reach for a bar of chocolate.
FRIEND: Did it do any good?
MAN: No, I can't get the chocolate to light.

Doctor, doctor, everyone keeps throwing me in the dustbin!
Don't talk rubbish.

Doctor, doctor, I think I'm an adder!
Great, you can help me with my accounts!

Doctor, doctor, I'm worried. This is the first time I've had an operation.
I know how you feel, it's the first time I've done one.

Doctor, doctor, how can I lose 15 kilos of fat?
How about cutting your head off?

MADGE: The doctor said I'm allergic to horses.
ETHEL: I've never heard of anyone suffering from that before. What's the condition called?
MADGE: Bronco-it-is.

Doctor, doctor, I'm so ugly. What can I do about it?
Hire yourself out for Hallowe'en parties.

Doctor, doctor, I think I'm turning into a mummy!
Hmm, better keep well wrapped up.

Doctor, doctor, my sister thinks she's a lift.
Well tell her to come in.
I can't, she doesn't stop at this floor.

Doctor, doctor, my family think I'm crazy!
Why on earth do they think that?
Because I like pork pies.
Well, I like pork pies, too.
Then you'll have to come round and see my collection. I've got thousands of them.

Did you hear about the plastic surgeon?
He sat in front of the fire and melted.

Doctor, doctor, the chemist said these pills you prescribed me are for cows.
Well, you said you wanted to be as strong as an ox.

Doctor, doctor, I'm really worried about my breathing.
Don't worry – we'll soon find something to stop it.

Doctor, you know those pills you gave me for B.O.?
Yes, Mr Pong?
They keep slipping out from under my arms!

Nurse, nurse, will the doctor be round soon?
No, he'll be tall and slim, as usual.

Doctor, doctor, my husband smells like a fish!
Poor sole!

Doctor, doctor, my baby's swallowed a watch.
Give it some epsom salts then, that should help it pass the time.

Doctor, doctor, I've had terrible tummy ache since I ate three crabs yesterday.
Did they smell bad when you took them out of their shells?
What do you mean, 'took them out of their shells'?

Doctor, doctor, I keep thinking I'm a roll of film.
Don't worry, I'm sure nothing will develop.

Doctor, doctor, what did the x-ray of my head show?
Absolutely nothing!

Doctor, doctor, I think I'm a billiard ball.
Sorry, you'll have to go to the end of the cue.

Doctor, doctor, I get so nervous when I drive that I keep bumping into things.
Don't worry, I'll prescribe a crash course.

Doctor, doctor, three beer kegs have just fallen on me!
Don't worry, it was light ale.

Doctor, doctor, I keep thinking I'm a nit!
Will you get out of my hair!

Old Bert couldn't look after himself any more so his kids put him in a nursing home. They chose the best nursing home that money could buy. Old Bert had the best room, the best food and two nurses who sat, one each side of his bed, 24 hours a day.

When his kids went to visit him they noticed that whenever Old Bert leaned to the left the nurse on the left would immediately straighten him up. And when he leaned to the right, that nurse would straighten him up too. This continued throughout the visit.

'Well, Dad, how do you like it here?' asked the eldest son.

'It would be fine if it wasn't for those two nurses,' grumbled Old Bert.

'What's wrong with them?' asked his son, puzzled.

'Every time I lean over to fart they won't let me!' retorted Old Bert.

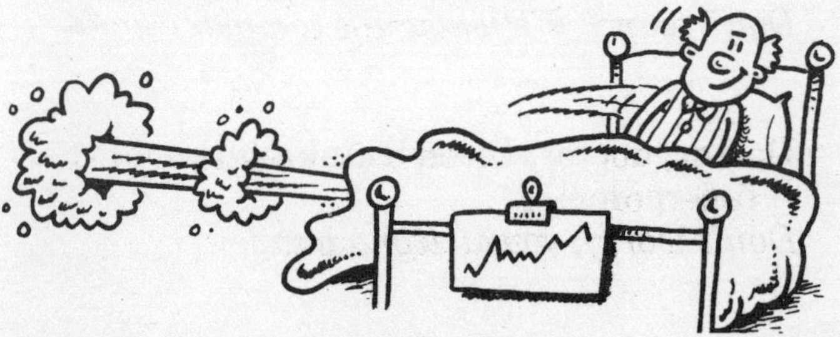

DOCTOR: You've got quite a nasty chill. You must avoid draughts for a week or two.
PATIENT: Can I play Ludo instead?

Doctor, doctor, I think I'm a moth!
So what made you come here, then?
Well, I saw this light at the window . . .

Doctor, doctor, I think I'm a rubber band!
Why don't you stretch yourself out on the couch and tell me all about it?

Doctor, doctor, my husband keeps dressing up like a French soldier!
Another case of legionnaire's disease.

Inscribed on the tomb of a hypochondriac:
I TOLD YOU I WAS ILL!

Doctor, doctor, I keep painting myself gold!
Don't worry, it's just a gilt complex.

Doctor, doctor, I keep thinking I'm a caterpillar!
Don't worry, you'll soon change.

Doctor, doctor, I'm shrinking!
Well, you'll just have to be a little patient.

MUM: Joe, it's time for your medicine.
JOE: I'll just run the bath.
MUM: Why?
JOE: Because on the bottle it says, 'To be taken in water.'

DOCTOR: Now just stand on the scales, please, madam. See, I told you that you were overweight. Just look at the chart.
PATIENT: No, I'm not. I'm just six inches too short.

FRANTIC PATIENT: Doctor, I've just swallowed a mouth organ!
DOCTOR: It could be worse, you could play the piano.

DOCTOR: Well, I've given you a thorough checkup and there's nothing wrong with you apart from lack of exercise. You must take a brisk walk of at least two miles every day.
PATIENT: I'll get very dizzy if I do that, doctor.
DOCTOR: Why on earth would walking make you dizzy?
PATIENT: I live in a lighthouse.

A doctor had just given a schoolboy a vaccination and was about to put a plaster on his arm.

'Would you put it on the other arm, please?' asked the boy.

'What's the point of that?' asked the doctor. 'If I put it over your vaccination the other boys will know not to bang it.'

'You don't know the kids in my school,' sighed the boy.

Anyone who goes to the psychiatrist wants his head examined.

Doctor, doctor, I keep thinking I'm a snail!
Don't worry, we'll soon have you out of your shell.

The doctor was surprised.
But when Old Macdonald had a farm
He couldn't believe his eyes!

A man went to the optician's to have his eyes tested. The optician sat him down and showed him a test page.

'Can you read that?' asked the optician.

'No,' said the man.

So the optician moved it closer. 'Can you read it now?'

'No,' said the man.

The optician moved it even closer.

'Surely you can read it now?' he asked.

'No,' said the man. 'I can't read.'

Doctor, doctor, I keep thinking I'm a butterfly!
Just say what you mean and stop flitting about!

Doctor, doctor, I've broken my arm in two places!
Well don't go back to them again.

A very plump lady went to see the doctor.
'I'm worried about my figure, doctor,' she said.
'You'll just have to diet,' the doctor told her.
'What colour?' asked the lady.

My brother's in hospital.
What's wrong with him?
He's got spotted fever.
Crikey! Is it serious?
No – it was spotted
in time.

A man went to the doctor's one day, complaining that he kept suffering from bad headaches. 'It's because I share a house with my two brothers,' he said.
'One of them has six goats and the other has four pigs and they all live in the house with us. The smell is terrible.'
'Well, why don't you open the windows?' said the doctor.
'I can't do that!' said the man. 'My bats might fly away.'

GRUESOME GHOULS

What do you call a monster that picks his nose?
The Bogeyman.

What do ghosts like in their coffee?
Evaporated milk.

What's a monster's favourite hobby?
Tie and die.

Did you hear about the horrible, hairy monster who did farmyard impressions?
He didn't do the noises he just made the smells.

What do you get when you cross a skunk with Frankenstein?
A Stinkenstein.

Where do vampire teachers come from?
Teacher Draining College.

How do you catch a vampire fish?
With blood worms

What is a vampire's favourite animal?
A giraffe – because it has such a long neck.

What do you get if you cross King Kong with a frog?
A gorilla that catches aeroplanes with its tongue.

How do you stop a werewolf from howling in the back of a car?
Put him in the front.

What's a vampire's favourite breed of dog?
A Bloodhound.

What do you call an overweight vampire?
Draculard.

Why do monsters let out bloodcurdling screams?
Because otherwise the blood would be too runny to spread on their sandwiches.

A werewolf can't die,
A vampire can fly,
A monster can bite off your head.
It's no wonder I'm scared
'Cos the noise I've just heard
Means they're all hiding under my bed!

What do you get if you cross a skeleton with peanut butter?
Extra crunchy peanut butter.

When do monsters eat eyeballs?
On fried-eyes.

What do you call a ghost's horse?
A nightmare.

What streets do ghosts haunt?
Dead ends.

What did the zombie get his medal for?
Deadication.

Why did the football coach bring a baby ghost to the game?
Because he wanted to show a little spirit.

What do you call a skeleton that refuses to do any work?
Bone idle.

Why wouldn't the postman deliver the ghost's letters?
He was on his coffin break.

What do you get if you cross a zombie with a boy scout?
A creature that scares old people across the road.

Why aren't robots afraid of monsters?
Because they have nerves of steel.

Which day of the week do ghosts like best?
Moan-days.

Why do vampire families never fight each other?
Because they can't stand bad blood.

Why did the monster take his nose apart?
To see what makes it run.

What do you do with a blue monster?
Try and cheer him up a bit.

Why did the witch keep turning people into Mickey Mouse?
She kept having Disney spells.

Who was the skeleton in the cupboard?
The winner of last year's hide and seek.

What do you get if you cross a witch with a telescope?
A horrorscope.

There was a huge monster from Leek,
Who, instead of a nose, had a beak,
It grew quite absurd,
Till he looked like a bird,
He migrates at the end of the week.

What do you call a sleeping monster that makes a lot of noise?
Frankensnore.

What don't zombies wear on boat trips?
Life jackets.

When a monster's hungry and wants
  to be fed,
It's no use hiding under your bed,
He'll roll you in the mattress,
Till you're buried like a mole,
Then chomp you up in two big bites,
Like a giant sausage roll.

What do you call a wizard from outer space?
A flying sorcerer.

What do you get if you cross a vampire with a mummy?
A flying bandage.

How do monsters get into your house?
With skeleton keys.

How do you know when a zombie is tired?
He's dead on his feet.

MOTHER MONSTER: Did you catch everyone's eyes in that pretty dress, dear?
GIRL MONSTER: Yes, Mum. And I've brought them home to play marbles with.

What is ugly, scary and very blue?
A vampire holding his breath.

What do you get if you cross a vampire with a flea?
Lots of very worried dogs.

What usually runs in witches' families?
Noses.

Why do skeletons always catch cold?
Because they get chilled to the bone.

What happened to Ray when he met the man-eating monster?
He became ex-Ray.

What do you get if you cross a vampire with a rose?
A flower that goes for your throat when you sniff it.

What do you call a skeleton who goes out in the snow and rain without a coat or umbrella?
A numbskull.

What sort of monster wakes you up in the morning with a nice cup of tea?
A mummy.

Which rooms don't zombies like?
Living rooms.

What do you get when you cross a werewolf with a dozen eggs?
A hairy omelette.

Why do skeletons frighten easily?
Because they haven't got any guts.

What do lady ghosts put on their skin?
Vanishing cream.

How do you make a skeleton laugh?
Tickle his funny bone.

What sort of music do mummies like best?
Wrap music.

Why do skeletons rub themselves all over with a towel when they've been swimming?
To get bone dry.

Did you hear about the witch who was caught speeding on her broomstick?
She had a brush with the law.

Why did the cannibal feel sick after eating the missionary?
Because you can't keep a good man down.

What goes out at night and goes chomp . . . suck . . . OUCH!
A vampire with a toothache.

What do you get if you cross a monster with a dog?
A neighbourhood without cats.

Why did the witch ride her broomstick on Hallowe'en?
So she could sweep the sky.

STINKY SCHOOL

My last school was so rough they didn't have a school photograph – they sent home identikit pictures instead.

We sent our teacher's photograph to a lonely hearts club.
They sent it straight back with a letter saying they weren't that lonely!

Our geography teacher is brilliant.
He has a broad knowledge of the subject.

Which schoolbooks help you get fit?
Exercise books.

Did you hear about the posh school where all the pupils smelt?
Only filthy rich kids went there.

What's the difference between teachers and chocolate?
Kids like chocolate.

RASHID: My sister's the school swot.
SONITA: Does she do well in exams?
RASHID: No, but she kills a lot of flies.

What is the dead centre of London?
The cemetery.

What's the difference between a boring teacher and a boring book?
You can shut the book up.

Did you hear about the schoolboy who couldn't do decimals?
He didn't see the point.

What's the difference between school dinners and a bucket of fresh manure?
School dinners are usually cold.

Where do new teachers come from?
They're produced on an assembly line.

Why is school like a shower?
One wrong turn and you're in hot water.

A warning to any young sinner:
If you do not repent,
To Hell you'll be sent,
With nothing to eat but school dinner.

TEACHER: I think you've been built upside down, Collins.
COLLINS: Why's that, sir?
TEACHER: Because your feet smell and your nose runs.

TEACHER: Williams, why are you taking those trainers into the examination room?
WILLIAMS: Because I want to jog my memory, sir.

When is an English teacher like a judge?
When she hands out long sentences.

Why is a classroom like an old car?
Because it's full of nuts and has a crank at the front.

What is the definition of a school report?
A poison pen letter from the headmaster.

TEACHER: Peter, why are you scratching yourself?
PETER: Because no one else knows where I itch.

TEACHER: I wish you'd pay a little attention.
GARY: I'm paying as little as possible.

I'm not saying our teacher's fat but every time he falls over he rocks himself to sleep trying to get back up.

Why did the school caretaker take early retirement?
Because he realised that grime doesn't pay.

Teacher's strong,
Teacher's gentle,
Teacher's kind,
And I am mental.

TEACHER: Now, Johnny, can you tell me what a circle is?
JOHNNY: Yes, miss. It's a round, straight line with a hole in the middle.

Why are art galleries like retirement homes for teachers?
Because they are full of old masters.

TEACHER: Now who can tell me what a Robin is?
CLEVER DICK: A bird that steals, sir.

TEACHER: Why are you picking your nose in class?
PUPIL: My mum won't let me pick it at home.

Two mice were talking in a science lesson.
FIRST MOUSE: I've got the science teacher well trained.
SECOND MOUSE: How have you done that?
FIRST MOUSE: I don't know, but every time I run through the maze and ring the bell he gives me a piece of cheese.

Why did the headmaster marry the school cleaner?
She swept him off his feet.

When is a blue school book not a blue school book?
When it is read.

What's black and white and horrible?
A maths examination paper.

Amy had just returned from a holiday in America.
TEACHER: Did you see the Catskill Mountains while you were in America?
AMY: No, but I saw them kill mice.

David's teacher was so fed up of him playing up in class that he wrote a letter to his parents.

'What's all this about?' yelled his father, waving the letter. 'Your teacher says it's impossible to teach you anything!'

'I told you he was no good,' said David.

What is the most popular sentence at school?
I don't know.

What does the music teacher do when he's locked out of his classroom?
Sings until he gets the right key.

I used to be thin,
Now I'm thinner,
So would you be,
With our school dinner!

TEACHER: Gary, wipe that mud off your shoes before you come into the classroom!
GARY: But, miss, I'm not wearing any shoes!

Did you hear about the Irish boy that had a soft spot for his science teacher?
It was a bog in the middle of Ireland.

Why was the cannibal expelled from school?
Because he kept buttering up the teacher.

What has eight feet and sings?
The school quartet.

What should a teacher take if he's run down?
The number of the car that hit him.

What happened to the baby chicken that misbehaved at school?
It was eggspelled.

TEACHER: Who can tell me what B.C. stands for?
SILLY SARA: Before Calculators.

What are pupils at ghost schools called?
Ghoulboys and ghoulgirls.

TEACHER: Do you know, Collins, that in the staffroom we call you the wonder boy?

COLLINS: Why's that, sir?

TEACHER: Because we all wonder when you're going to take a bath.

The teacher was telling the class about all the different sorts of birds and their various habits.

'Now, does anyone know the names of any birds who don't build their own nests?' she asked.

Sam put up his hand. 'The cuckoo, miss!'

'Very good, Sam,' smiled the teacher. 'How did you know that?'

'Because cuckoos live in clocks,' replied Sam.

KATE: Our teacher has what you call a sympathetic face.

STEVE: What do you mean?

KATE: People look at him and feel sympathetic.

A little boy came home from his first day at school and said to his mother, 'What's the use of going to school? I can't read, I can't write and the teacher won't let me talk!'

TEACHER: How can we stop polluting our waters?

ANNIE: Stop taking baths?

TEACHER (to dinner lady): A pork chop, please, and make it lean.
DINNER LADY: Certainly, Mr Smith. Which way?

Did you hear about the teacher who married the dairy maid?
It didn't last long. They were like chalk and cheese.

Miss Smith who teaches us maths,
Isn't a bundle of laughs,
For, sad to tell,
She doesn't half smell,
For she has never taken a bath.

A teacher started off the lesson saying, 'Now I want you all to give me a list of the lower animals, starting with Georgina Clark.'

TEACHER: I'd like to go through one whole day without having to tell you off, Jones.
JONES: I wish you would, sir!

What is brown, wears dark glasses and carries a pile of exercise books?
A coconut disguised as a teacher.

TEACHER: You weren't at school last Friday, Robert. I heard you were out playing football all day.
ROBERT: That's not true, sir. And I've got the cinema tickets to prove it.

NAUSEATING KNOCK KNOCKS

Knock, knock.
Who's there?
Sonia.
Sonia who?
Sonia shoe. I can smell it from here!

Knock, knock.
Who's there?
Phew.
Phew who?
Phew, there's an awful smell around here. Is it you?

Knock, knock.
Who's there?
Gopher.
Gopher who?
Gopher a walk over the cliff!

knock.
here?

ho?
e questions around here!

knock.
:here?

ho?
. Elastic!

knock.
there?

who?
plays, nights he sleeps!

knock.
there?

who?
alk with your mouth full!

knock.
there?

who?
your business!

Knock, knock.
Who's there?
Giraffe.
Giraffe who?
Giraffe to sit in front of me at the cinema?

Knock, knock.
Who's there?
Phillipa.
Phillipa who?
Phillipa bath, I'm very dirty!

Knock, knock.
Who's there?
Crispin.
Crispin who?
Crispin crunchy frog sandwiches!

Knock, knock.
Who's there?
Adair.
Adair who?
Adair once but
I'm bald now!

Knock, knock.
Who's there?
Al.
Al who?
Al give you a kiss if you open the door!

Knock, knock.
Who's there?
Scott.
Scott who?
It's got nothing to do with you!

Knock, knock.
Who's there?
Paul Aidy.
Paul Aidy who?
Paul Aidy who just fell in the cow dung!

Knock, knock.
Who's there?
Canoe.
Canoe who?
Canoe come out and play today?

Knock, knock.
Who's there?
Albert.
Albert who?
Albert you don't know who this is!

Knock, knock.
Who's there?
Yul.
Yul who?
Yul never know if you don't open the door, w

Knock, knock.
Who's there?
Kipper.
Kipper who?
Kipper your hands to yourself!

Knock, knock.
Who's there?
Dummy.
Dummy who?
Dummy a favour and open the door!

Knock,
Who's
Alex.
Alex w
Alex th

Knock,
Who's
Nick.
Nick w
Nick R

Knock,
Who's
Daisy.
Daisy
Daisy

Knock
Who's
Dana.
Dana
Dana

Knock
Who's
Nona.
Nona
Nona

Knock, knock.
Who's there?
Corah.
Corah who?
Corah wish I had a front door like this!

Knock, knock.
Who's there?
Twitter.
Twitter who?
Have you got an owl in there?

Knock, knock.
Who's there?
Cilla.
Cilla who?
The Cilla beggar who's forgotten her key again!

Knock, knock.
Who's there?
Allied.
Allied who?
Allied, so sue me!

Knock, knock.
Who's there?
Geezer.
Geezer who?
Geezer couple of minutes and I'll pick the lock!

Knock, knock.
Who's there?
Alpaca.
Alpaca who?
Alpaca the trunk, you pack the suitcase!

Knock, knock.
Who's there?
Ivor.
Ivor who?
Ivor key of my own now!

Knock, knock.
Who's there?
Avenue.
Avenue who?
Avenue guessed yet?

Knock, knock.
Who's there?
Tristan.
Tristan who?
Tristan insect to really get up your nose!

Knock, knock.
Who's there?
Amana.
Amana who?
Amana bad mood!

Knock, knock.
Who's there?
Underwear.
Underwear who?
Underwear my key is tonight?

Knock, knock.
Who's there?
Luke.
Luke who?
Luke, stop messing about and let me in!

Knock, knock.
Who's there?
Ivor.
Ivor who?
Ivor got my fingers stuck in your letter box!

Knock, knock.
Who's there?
Lucy.
Lucy who?
Lucy Lastic can be embarrassing!

Knock, knock.
Who's there?
Berlin.
Berlin who?
Berlin the water for my hard-boiled eggs!

Knock, knock.
Who's there?
Luke.
Luke who?
Luke through the little spyglass and you'll see!

Knock, knock.
Who's there?
Ellie.
Ellie who?
Ellie Funt.

Knock, knock.
Who's there?
Brewster.
Brewster who?
Brewster can wake you up in the morning singing cock-a-doodle-do!

Knock, knock.
Who's there?
Gladys.
Gladys who?
Gladys nice weather if you're going to keep me waiting out here all day!

Knock, knock.
Who's there?
Arbus.
Arbus who?
Arbus leaves in five minutes!

Knock, knock.
Who's there?
Anka.
Anka who?
Anka the ship!

Knock, knock.
Who's there?
Brewster.
Brewster who?
Brewster can wake you up in the morning singing cock-a-doodle-do!

Knock, knock.
Who's there?
Gladys.
Gladys who?
Gladys nice weather if you're going to keep me waiting out here all day!

Knock, knock.
Who's there?
Arbus.
Arbus who?
Arbus leaves in five minutes!

Knock, knock.
Who's there?
Anka.
Anka who?
Anka the ship!

Knock, knock.
Who's there?
Luke.
Luke who?
Luke through the little spyglass and you'll see!

Knock, knock.
Who's there?
Ellie.
Ellie who?
Ellie Funt.

Knock, knock.
Who's there?
Underwear.
Underwear who?
Underwear my key is tonight?

Knock, knock.
Who's there?
Luke.
Luke who?
Luke, stop messing about and let me in!

Knock, knock.
Who's there?
Ivor.
Ivor who?
Ivor got my fingers stuck in your letter box!

Knock, knock.
Who's there?
Lucy.
Lucy who?
Lucy Lastic can be embarrassing!

Knock, knock.
Who's there?
Berlin.
Berlin who?
Berlin the water for my hard-boiled eggs!

Knock, knock.
Who's there?
Alpaca.
Alpaca who?
Alpaca the trunk, you pack the suitcase!

Knock, knock.
Who's there?
Ivor.
Ivor who?
Ivor key of my own now!

Knock, knock.
Who's there?
Avenue.
Avenue who?
Avenue guessed yet?

Knock, knock.
Who's there?
Tristan.
Tristan who?
Tristan insect to really get up your nose!

Knock, knock.
Who's there?
Amana.
Amana who?
Amana bad mood!

Knock, knock.
Who's there?
Cilla.
Cilla who?
The Cilla beggar who's forgotten her key again!

Knock, knock.
Who's there?
Allied.
Allied who?
Allied, so sue me!

Knock, knock.
Who's there?
Geezer.
Geezer who?
Geezer couple of minutes and I'll pick the lock!

Knock, knock.
Who's there?
Corah.
Corah who?
Corah wish I had a front door like this!

Knock, knock.
Who's there?
Twitter.
Twitter who?
Have you got an owl in there?

Knock, knock.
Who's there?
Giraffe.
Giraffe who?
Giraffe to sit in front of me at the cinema?

Knock, knock.
Who's there?
Phillipa.
Phillipa who?
Phillipa bath, I'm very dirty!

Knock, knock.
Who's there?
Crispin.
Crispin who?
Crispin crunchy frog sandwiches!

Knock, knock.
Who's there?
Adair.
Adair who?
Adair once but
I'm bald now!

Knock, knock.
Who's there?
Al.
Al who?
Al give you a kiss if you open the door!

Knock, knock.
Who's there?
Scott.
Scott who?
It's got nothing to do with you!

Knock, knock.
Who's there?
Paul Aidy.
Paul Aidy who?
Paul Aidy who just fell in the cow dung!

Knock, knock.
Who's there?
Canoe.
Canoe who?
Canoe come out and play today?

Knock, knock.
Who's there?
Albert.
Albert who?
Albert you don't know
who this is!

Knock, knock.
Who's there?
Yul.
Yul who?
Yul never know if you
don't open the door, will you?

Knock, knock.
Who's there?
Kipper.
Kipper who?
Kipper your hands
to yourself!

Knock, knock.
Who's there?
Dummy.
Dummy who?
Dummy a favour
and open the door!

Knock, knock.
Who's there?
Alex.
Alex who?
Alex the questions around here!

Knock, knock.
Who's there?
Nick.
Nick who?
Nick R. Elastic!

Knock, knock.
Who's there?
Daisy.
Daisy who?
Daisy plays, nights he sleeps!

Knock, knock.
Who's there?
Dana.
Dana who?
Dana talk with your mouth full!

Knock, knock.
Who's there?
Nona.
Nona who?
Nona your business!

Knock, knock.
Who's there?
Whoopi.
Whoopi who?
Whoopi cushion!

Knock, knock.
Who's there?
Ben.
Ben who?
Ben knocking on this door all morning!

Knock, knock.
Who's there?
Betty!
Betty who?
Betty ya don't know who this is!

Knock, knock.
Who's there?
Boliva.
Boliva who?
Boliva me, I know what I'm talking about!

Knock, knock.
Who's there?
Deena.
Deena who?
Deena hear me the first time?

Knock, knock.
Who's there?
Voodoo.
Voodoo who?
Voodoo you think you are?

Knock, knock.
Who's there?
Arthur.
Arthur who?
Arthur any more biscuits in the tin?

Knock, knock.
Who's there?
Plaice.
Plaice who?
Plaice let me in, I'm wet through!

Knock, knock.
Who's there?
Aliens.
Aliens who?
Just how many aliens do you know?

Knock, knock.
Who's there?
Sacha.
Sacha who?
Sacha lot of questions in this exam!

Knock, knock.
Who's there?
Colleen.
Colleen who?
Colleen yourself up, you look filthy!

Knock, knock.
Who's there?
Butter.
Butter who?
Butter bring an umbrella,
it looks like it might rain!

Knock, knock.
Who's there?
De Niro.
De Niro who?
De Niro I am to you,
the more I like you!

Knock, knock.
Who's there?
Atomic.
Atomic who?
Atomic ache!

Knock, knock.
Who's there?
McKee.
McKee who?
McKee doesn't fit!

Knock, knock.
Who's there?
Donalette.
Donalette who?
Donalette the bed bugs bite!

Knock, knock.
Who's there?
Duane.
Duane who?
Duane the bath, I'm dwowning!

Knock, knock.
Who's there?
Rufus.
Rufus who?
Rufus leaking and I'm getting wet!

Knock, knock.
Who's there?
Hali.
Hali who?
Halitosis – your breath smells awful!

Knock, knock.
Who's there?
Disc.
Disc who?
Disc is a recorded message, please leave your message after the bleep!

Knock, knock.
Who's there?
Irish Stew.
Irish Stew who?
Irish Stew in the name of the law!

Knock, knock.
Who's there?
Jester.
Jester who?
Jester minute – this is my house. What are you doing in there?

Knock, knock.
Who's there?
Howard.
Howard who?
Howard you like to stand out here in the cold while some idiot keeps saying, 'Who's there?'

Knock, knock.
Who's there?
Ida.
Ida who?
I'd an awful time at school today!

Knock, knock.
Who's there?
Zombie.
Zombie who?
Zombies make honey, others are Queens!

Knock, knock.
Who's there?
Amos.
Amos who?
A mosquito just bit me!

Knock, knock.
Who's there?
Andy.
Andy who?
Andy mosquito bit me again!

Knock, knock.
Who's there?
Noah.
Noah who?
Noah good place to eat?

Knock, knock.
Who's there?
Amsterdam.
Amsterdam who?
Amsterdam tired of all these knock knock jokes!

PUTRID PUNS

How do you keep flies out of the kitchen?
Put a bucket of manure in the lounge.

What happened to the man who swallowed a door knob?
It turned his stomach.

What type of ball can't you play with?
An eyeball.

What do you call a man who keeps a wild ferret down his pants?
Very, very stupid.

Where does a sick ship go?
To the dock.

What's red and stupid?
A blood clot.

MAN (tucking into a sandwich): This beef is nice and warm.
WIFE: So it should be. The cat's been sitting on it all day.

If you really loved me,
You'd let me call you Jack,
Then you could lift up my car,
And mend the puncture at the back.

How do you make someone burn their ear?
Ring them up while they're ironing.

What's white on the outside, green on the inside and hops?
A frog sandwich.

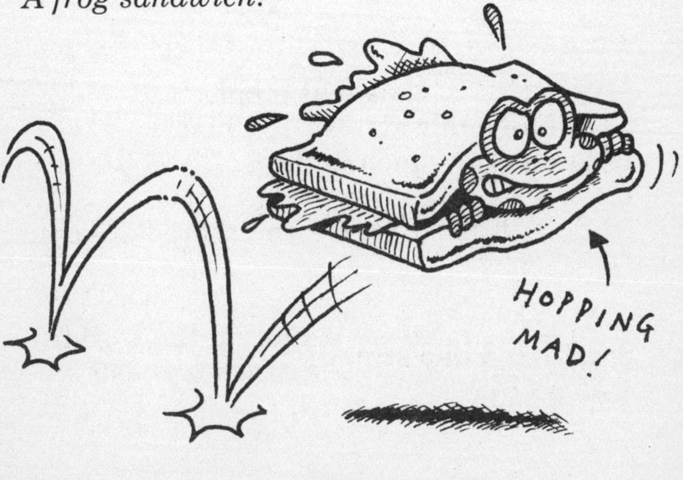

What do you call your brother's smelly son?
My ne-phew.

A man went into a chemist shop and asked for a spray that would make his room smell like rotten eggs, smelly socks and sour milk.

'Why on earth do you want your room to smell like that?' asked the chemist.

'Because I'm leaving today and my landlord said I have to leave my flat how I found it,' said the man.

TOM: Why do you suck your maggots before putting them on the hook?
SAM: So I can wait for the fish with baited breath.

A man that's as bald as a bat,
Spilt hair tonic all over the mat.
It's grown so much higher,
He can't see the fire,
And he thinks that it's smothered the cat.

Who is the meanest person in the world?
A man who finds a sling then breaks his arm so he can wear it.

What has one head, one foot and four legs?
A bed.

How do you make scotch eggs?
Feed your chicken whisky.

Waiter, waiter, there's a maggot in my salad!
Don't worry, sir, it won't live long in that stuff.

BERTHA: My little brother can play the piano by ear.
BERT: So what? My little sister fiddles with her toes.

What happened when two fat men ran in a race?
One ran in short bursts and the other ran in burst shorts.

Why was the fat man run over by the
steam roller?
To prove that he had lots of guts.

How did the farmer fix his ripped jeans?
With a cabbage patch.

How do you make milk shake?
Give it a good scare.

Why did the boy put sugar on his pillow?
So he would have sweet dreams.

NEIGHBOUR (peering over the fence):
What are you going to do with that pile
of manure?
MAN: Put it on my strawberries.
NEIGHBOUR: Really? I put cream on mine.

Why did the doll blush?
Because she saw the teddy bare.

HAROLD: I live on garlic alone.
TED: Anyone who lives on garlic should live alone.

How can you make a thin person fat?
Push him over a cliff and he'll come down plump.

Where do Martians drink beer?
At a mars bar.

I went to the pictures tomorrow,
I had a front seat at the back,
I had a plain cake with currants,
I ate it and give it her back.

What runs but never walks?
Water.

Where do astronauts leave their spaceships?
At parking meteors.

Why did the hazelnut go out with a prune?
Because he couldn't find a date.

What does one star say to another star?
Glad to meteor.

What happens if you eat yeast and shoe polish?
You'll rise and shine in the morning.

What goes into the water pink and comes out blue?
A swimmer on a cold day.

What lives on a ship and says, 'Croak! Croak!' when it's foggy?
A froghorn.

What did the silly girl buy when the joke shop ran out of itching powder?
A scratch card.

Why is a christmas tree like a bad knitter?
They both drop their needles.

There was a young man from Dunbarton,
Who thought he could run like a Spartan,
On the thirty-ninth lap,
His braces went snap,
And his face went a red Scottish tartan.

What happens if you play table tennis with a bad egg?
It goes ping, then it goes pong.

What can you put in a barrel that makes it lighter?
Holes.

Why did the man put a shoe by his ear?
He wanted to listen to sole music.

Caveman chases dinosaur,
Fancies a bronto burger,
Hungry T-Rex joins in too,
How he enjoys human stew!

What Spanish dance do people do at the end of the summer?
The tan-go.

What's the smelliest city in America?
Phew York.

What's grey and zooms through the jungle at 70 miles an hour?
An elephant on a motorbike.

The seaside we went to last week was so boring that one day the tide went out and didn't come back.

Why did the man have butterflies in his stomach?
Because he swallowed some caterpillars.

What has two legs, one wheel and stinks like mad?
A wheelbarrow full of manure.

Mummy, mummy, why can't we have a dustbin?
Shut up and keep chewing!

What's long, orange and wears nappies?
A baby carrot.

What's black, rushes out of the ground and shouts 'excuse me'?
Refined oil.

What do you call a flying policeman?
A helicopper.

Humpty Dumpty sat on the wall,
Humpty Dumpty had a great fall,
All the King's horses,
And all the King's men,
Had scrambled eggs for supper again!

What's green, has four legs and two trunks?
Two seasick tourists.

What is cowhide most used for?
Holding cows together.

I have two noses, three eyes and only one ear. What am I?
Very ugly.

What will happen if you put jelly in the toaster?
It'll jam.

What is the dirtiest word in the world?
Pollution.

What did the banana sitting in the sun say to the other banana?
I don't know about you but I'm starting to peel.

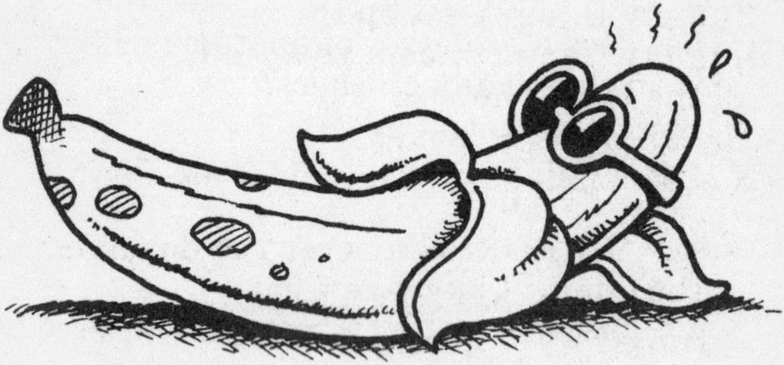

Did you hear about the karate champion who joined the army?
The first time he saluted he nearly killed himself.

WAITER: Sorry, sir, the soup is off today.
MAN: I should say it is, mine's covered in green mould.

Why did the idiot have his sundial floodlit?
So he could tell the time at night.

Why is it difficult to open a piano?
Because all the keys are inside.

Why are martians green?
Because they forgot to take their travel sickness tablets.

What does a professor of anatomy eat with cheese and crackers?
Pickled organs.

SNOOTY WOMAN: Whenever I'm down in the dumps I buy a new hat.
EVEN SNOOTIER FRIEND: So that's where you get them!

Why did the tree go to the dentist?
To get a root canal.

Why did the boy become an astronaut?
Because he was no earthly good.

Why did the atom cross the road?
Because it was time to split.

SUE: My boyfriend reminds me of the sea.
KATE: How? Is he strong, exciting and full of surprises?
SUE: No – he makes me feel sick!

When is water musical?
When it's piping hot.

Which hand should you use to stir your tea?
Neither, you should use a spoon.

What did the ground say to the earthquake?
You crack me up.

Did you hear about the sword swallower who swallowed an umbrella?
He wanted to put something away for a rainy day.

How can you see stars in the daytime?
Hit yourself on the head.

A little old lady went to stay at a huge hotel in Texas. The lady was amazed how big everything in the hotel was. She went to the café for a drink and told the waitress that she'd never seen anything as big as the hotel or her suite.

'Everything's big in Texas, ma'am,' said the waitress.

The waitress soon returned with a coffee in the biggest cup the old lady had ever seen.

'I told you, ma'am, everything's big in Texas,' said the waitress, seeing the old lady's astonishment.

On the way back to her suite the lady got lost in the vast corridors. She opened the door of a dark room and fell into an enormous swimming pool.

'Please!' she screamed. 'Don't flush it!'

Roses are red,
Violets are blue,
You look like a pig,
And you smell like one, too!

What's black and white, pongs and hangs from a line?
A drip-dry skunk.

DARREN: I'm so tired I feel like an old sock.
SUSAN: I thought there was a funny smell around here.